# The Astronomer
## Caroline Herschel
### A Short Biography

By Doug West, Ph.D.

C&D Publications

The Astronomer Caroline Herschel
A Short Biography
By Doug West, Ph.D.

ISBN: 9798378603527

# Table of Contents

# Preface

Welcome to the book, *The Astronomer Caroline Herschel: A Short Biography*. This book is volume 66 of the 30 Minute Book Series, and as the name of the series implies, if you are an average reader this book should take less than an hour to read. Since this short book is not meant to be an all-encompassing biography of Caroline Herschel, you may want to know more about her life and times. To help you with this, there are several good references at the end of this book. I have also provided a Timeline, in order to link together the important events in her life, and a section of the book titled "Biographical Sketches," which includes brief biographies of some of the key individuals in the book. In the text, those individuals who are in one of the biographical sketches will have their name in **bold** print the first time they appear in the book.

Thank you for purchasing this book. I hope you enjoy your time reading about this pioneering female astronomer.

Doug West

February 2023

DOUG WEST, PH.D.

# Introduction

The Herschel family in 18th century Hanover, which is now part of Germany, was not a prominent or wealthy family. The father worked as a musician in the military, and his wife ran the household and raised their children—rather typical for that time and place. Out of that rather typical family came two siblings who changed the world of astronomy. **William**, the second oldest son, and Caroline, the youngest daughter, worked together to form one of the most important family legacies in the history of astronomy.

William, best known for his discovery of the planet Uranus, taught his younger sister how to use the telescope, record astronomical observations, and make the necessary mathematical calculations to reduce the observations so they would be useful for other astronomers. Though Caroline had only gone to school until she was 14 years old, she was a quick study and before long she knew her way around the night sky, making important discoveries on her own, including several comets.

Caroline's meticulous nature and attention to detail made her a natural at cataloging the thousands of observations the brother and sister team took over the decades. She also used her skill to make hundreds of corrections to Astronomer Royal **John Flamsteed's** star catalog, the best in the world at the time. Her work was recognized with a gold medal by the Royal Astronomical Society of Great Britain.

After the death of her brother, she assisted his son, **John Herschel**, by compiling a catalog of over 2,500 nebulae into a useful format. John took this nebula catalog with him to South Africa and spent four years making observations of the southern sky, correcting and adding to the catalog of nebulae.

Caroline Herschel was a remarkable woman who overcame many personal and physical obstacles to make a significant impact on the field of astronomy. Her determination and talent, combined with her close collaboration with her brother, enabled her to make numerous important discoveries and advances that helped shape the field of astronomy into what we know today. She stands as an inspiration, particularly to young women, of a person who overcame the many trials of life to pursue a career in science.

This is the story of a woman of humble origin who became one of the most notable astronomers of her day. This short biography covers the life and times of Caroline Herschel from cradle to grave.

# Chapter 1 - Early Years

Caroline Lucretia Herschel was born on March 16, 1750, in the Electorate of Hanover, a territory in the Holy Roman Empire. Of the 10 children of her parents Isaac and Anna Herschel, only six survived into adulthood, two girls and four boys. Caroline had one sister named Sophia who was nearly 17 years older and left the house for marriage when Caroline was young. With Sophia gone, Caroline became the only daughter at home, and her mother heavily depended on her to help with household chores from a young age.

Caroline's health was frail as a young girl. When she was four years old, she contracted smallpox, leaving one of her eyes disfigured and her face covered with pock marks. At age ten, she came down with typhus, which led to stunted growth to a height of 4'3". Her father was kind but realistic, and she later recorded his opinion on her prospects for marriage and family: "Against all thoughts of marrying, saying as I was neither handsome nor rich, it was not likely that anyone would make me an offer, till perhaps, when far advanced in life, some old man might take me for my good qualities" (Hoskins, 2007, p. 94). Life in Hanover was far from pleasant for the young Caroline Herschel.

Caroline's father and her two older brothers, William and Jacob, were all musicians in the Hanoverian Guard. During times of peace the requirements of duty were light, allowing the men to spend time at home. During times of war, they were required to march with the troops and suffer the same hardships as the soldiers. When Caroline was barely six, the men in the family were called to war as the French were threatening an invasion of England during the winter of 1755-1756. This was one of the opening acts of what would become known as the Seven Years War. Both Hanover and England were under the reign of King George II, and the soldiers of the Hanoverian Guard were called to England for a short time to act as reinforcements.

After their brief stay in England, Jacob was able to obtain a discharge and returned to Hanover to work as a musician in the Hanoverian Court Orchestra. William and Isaac returned to Hanover with their regiment. The following year the French attacked the English controlled state of Hanover. After the Hanoverian Guard suffered a bruising defeat at the Battle of Hastenbeck, the French occupied Hanover. The death and destruction resulting from the war caused Isaac to worry about the safety of his family. Since William was a teenager—a boy bandsman and not under oath—Isaac sent him back to Hanover to defend the city against the French. However, Anna realized it was safer for him back with his regiment as a non-combatant than to be a solider fighting the French at home. Thus William was able to quietly return to his unit without any complications.

As the fighting continued, Isaac insisted that William flee the conflict for the safety of England. William was able to avoid capture by the French and to meet up with Jacob, and the pair sailed for the relative safety of England. There, both young men found work as musicians. Jacob returned to Hanover when peace was restored but William, who had been labeled a deserter back in Hanover, remained in England to make his fortune as a musician. After years of struggle as a musician, William was able to land a favorable position as an organist at the exclusive Octagon Chapel in the resort town of Bath.

Figure – Map of Europe circa 1750.

## Caroline's Life in Hanover

Isaac Herschel wanted all of his children to be trained in mathematics, French, and music, and all were given opportunities, except for frail Caroline. Her mother, Anna, disapproved of her having an education; rather, she had simple plans for her daughter, believing educating Caroline was unnecessary because she would never marry and would be better off working as their house servant. Like the other children, Caroline attended the local Garrison School until the age of 14 for a basic education. Caroline's future in Hanover was bleak; she had little hope of a marriage or a career and seemed destined to be her mother's unpaid domestic servant.

As a young girl Anna kept Caroline very busy. After school ended during the middle of the afternoon, Anna put her to work knitting. When she was eight, after the end of the French occupation of Hanover, she helped her mother earn extra money by mending the tents and linen required by the troops. As Caroline grew into a teenager, her prospects for learning a skill that would allow her to work outside the family grew dim. One possible career option for a daughter from a working-class family was to work as a governess for a wealthy family. However, this would require her to teach the children in her charge the French language, of which Caroline knew little. In one of her autobiographies written in her later life, Caroline describes her family life as a young girl and her mother's hindrance of her education:

"For, he [Isaac] in consequence was not only deprived of leisure, but even the means for giving us such an education as he had intended, and about the manner of which my parents were of different opinions. My mother would not consent to my being taught French, and my brother Dietrich was even denied a dancing master because she would not permit my learning along with him though the entrance had been paid for us both; so all my father could do for me was to indulge me (and please himself) sometimes with a short lesson on the violin; when my mother was either in good humor or out of the way" (Hoskins, 2003, p. 34).

In the spring of 1760 Isaac returned home from war a broken man. The deprivations of the harsh conditions of the military camps had taken a toll on his health. In August 1764, Isaac suffered a stroke and only partially recovered. As a result, his ability to work was limited, and the family had to depend more on the money Jacob could bring to the family.

## William's Visit to Hanover

While William was making his way in England, Jacob was able to secure an honorable discharge for his brother from the Hanoverian Guard, thus allowing him to return to Hanover for a visit. In March 1764, Caroline was at what would normally be a much anticipated turning point in her life, able to leave school and focus on a career or seek a husband and family. Caroline had none of these to look forward to; however, one bright spot in her life was that after many years away, her beloved brother William was returning for a visit. Like her father, William had shown her kindness and held a special place in her heart. Unfortunately for Caroline, at the scheduled time of William's visit, she was planning to be very busy going through Confirmation at her church and wrapping up the requirements for the end of her education.

On April 2, 1764, William returned home for a short visit. Her brother's visit was a time of mixed feelings for Caroline, as she wanted to spend time with her brother but her mother's constant demands, the completion of her formal education, and the Confirmation at church took time away from seeing him. She later wrote of the joy her family felt with William being at home again:

"The first few days after my brother's arrival, our family was in a continual tumult of joy; of which however only a small portion could fall to my share for as none were willing to lose sight of him for a moment, I was obliged to be almost intirely absent from the groope, either to fetch or carry something, or attend at school and church, as the following Sunday I was to be confirmed. But by the few opportunities I could have to be present when my father was in conversation with my brother W$^m$, I learned soon that our joy of having him amongst us would be but of short duration..." (Hoskin, 2003, p. 36).

Caroline then tells how she realized her father would probably never see William again, and writes of her sadness that when he departed she was not able to tell him goodbye due to her obligation at church for her

Confirmation, "...My father's state of health would not allow him to comfort himself with the hope of another meeting; the joy of seeing a Son so dear was it may easily be conceived much embittered by the approaching moment of parting—which moment most unhappily for me was on the Sunday when I was to join the confirmed children at the Communion Table, where I was nearly annihilated by the Postilion's [coach driver's] horn as passing close to the Church door (at 11 o'clock) bearing away my dear Brother from whom I had been obliged to take leave at 8 o'Clock" (Hoskins, 2003, p. 36).

At age 17, Caroline's father died, and Jacob assumed the role of dictatorial head of the household. Isaac's death was devastating to her since he was the one resident family member who cared for her wellbeing and education. That summer, her brothers Jacob and Dietrich traveled to Bath to visit William. With two of her brothers gone from the house, Caroline's duties were light, allowing her to leave home for a couple of months to learn millinery (hat making). Jacob, who now assumed the role of man-of-the-house, agreed on the condition that she was to limit herself to making her own hats.

With her two brothers Dietrich and Jacob both in Bath, Caroline spent the winter of 1768-1769 practicing her newly acquired skills in needlework. Jacob found work as a musician in Bath and took his younger brother Dietrich along to train him as a musician. At the end of July 1769, both Jacob and Dietrich returned from Bath.

This greatly increased Caroline's workload around the house to the point where their mother hired a servant to help. The living quarters were so cramped that Caroline had to share a bed with the servant, which she much detested.

While William was living in Leeds, he boarded with the Bulman family. He found the arrangement so agreeable that when he moved to Bath he secured Mr. Bulman a position and invited the family to join him. Mrs. Bulman and her daughter ran the household but did not help William with his personal accounts or with his musical career.

Jacob visited William for a second time in 1770, this time taking with him Alexander, who settled in Bath until he retired to Hanover in 1816. William and Alexander were both aware of the way their mother mistreated Caroline and made plans to rescue her from their mother. William had hoped that Caroline could help him in the music profession, thus freeing her from the tyranny of her mother.

Though all the boys in the family were excellent musicians, Caroline had been excluded from the instruction given by Isaac. Not receiving any formal voice training, Caroline took it upon herself to learn as much as she could and practiced singing in the house when she had it all to herself. The two brothers were going to approach their mother with a plan to train Caroline as a singer so she could work with them in their performances. Chances were small that this shy German girl who knew no English could be trained to perform in front of an aristocratic audience on some of England's finest stages, but this was their excuse for needing Caroline in Bath.

In October 1771, a letter arrived from William proposing that Caroline pay an extended visit to Bath to see if she could be transformed into a soloist suitable for an English orchestra. Caroline was elated with the proposal and so was Jacob at first, but his opinion quickly turned to ridicule. William arrived in Hanover in early August 1772 to gain Caroline's release from her role as household drudge. Fortunately for Caroline, Jacob was away on duty with the Court Orchestra and was not involved with the decision. Anna was reluctant to lose her servant but relinquished when William promised an annual annuity to offset the loss.

# Chapter 2 -
# Caroline in England

During their journey to Bath, Caroline was surprised to learn of William's growing fascination with astronomy. While traveling through Holland in an open coach at night, William pointed out the constellations to her. Caroline was growing more convinced of her brother's new obsession when they traveled through London and stopped at optician's shops.

Arriving in Bath in late August, Caroline hoped to have a joyous reunion with her brother Alexander. This was not to be as he was away for a musical engagement for the summer. William immediately began to integrate Caroline into his household with the Bulman family. Caroline found Mrs. Bulman tolerable but their daughter, about Caroline's age, she found to be "very little better than an idiot."

William began his sister's music lessons in short order. He also taught her arithmetic, which girls were not normally taught in Hanover, so she could manage his personal affairs. Each Sunday she was given a sum of money for the weekly expenses and was expected to make an accounting of the money. For the first couple of months William gave her two to three music lessons per day. This quickly changed in the winter months when William's musical engagements began to take up all his time. To get in at least one lesson per day, Caroline got up early and sang to William while he ate breakfast. She wrote of her dilemma, "But the Season for public business being nearly at an end, because after the beginning of June Bath becomes intirely empty I hoped and expected my Brother would now help me on a little more in my Musical practice; and He was still pleased with my Voice but gave me [no] encouragement for bestowing much time in attempting to became a proficient player on the Harpsichord...About this time it was that my Brother began to give up much of his time to polishing Mirrors..." (Hoskin, 2003, p. 123).

For the next many years this would be William's pattern. During the winter months when music was in season, he devoted his time and attention to music; during the summer months the demand for musicians waned and he devoted as much time as he could spare to telescope making and the study of the night sky. William kept Caroline busy helping him with his dual interests. While he polished mirrors for his telescopes, which required hours of hand work, she would read to him or serve him food so he could work without interruption. She later recalled: "...by way of keeping him alife I was even obliged to feed him by putting the Vitals by bitts into his mouth—this was once the case when at the finishing of a 7 feet mirror he had not left his hands from it for 16 hours together...And generally I was obliged to read to him when at some work which required no thinking, and sometimes lending a hand" (Brock, p. 93).

Figure – Caroline assisting William in
the grinding of a telescope mirror.

On Sunday mornings and evenings, she helped William
with the chapel choir. Wednesday and Saturday
mornings she spent shopping and in the afternoons at
dance class. During the "season," from August until
Easter, the city of Bath came alive with visitors from all
over the country. They came to enjoy the warm mineral
baths and the lively musical and theatrical venues
throughout the city. During that time, William was fully
consumed by his music, and consequently so was
Caroline. William built her a special desk so she could

copy the innumerable sheets of music required by the orchestra and choristers standing up, so as not to infringe upon her voice. Although William was consumed by his own pursuits, he did not totally divest himself from Caroline's musical training. He paid for her dancing lessons and spent a considerable amount on a dress suitable for performances on a fashionable stage. During the winter of 1783-1784, William paid for her to travel to London to attend the performances of some of the best soloists in Britain.

## Caroline's Short-Lived Musical Career

In the spring of 1777, Caroline's musical career began to blossom. In March she sang for the first time as principal in a performance of Handel's *Judas Maccabaeus*, with two additional performances later that month. The following spring, she was the first soloist in Handel's *Messiah*. In the space of a few short years, Caroline had made an impressive, Cinderella-like ascendance from a German household drudge to an English soloist on par with some of the most trained voices Britain had to offer.

The public was taking notice of her skill as a singer. After one performance, she was approached by an audience member requesting she sing in a concert held in Birmingham. This was the big break she had been hoping for. Unfortunately, it came with a cost she was not willing to accept: she would have to be gone for several days, away from William and her home. Becoming an independent woman scared her. She had always performed with William as the conductor, and the engagement in Birmingham would require her to be on her own for several days or more and be the center of attention.

When the moment of decision came, she realized she was not ready to leave her home and family, stating, "I never intended to sing anywhere but where my Brother was the conductor." This was a turning point for her personally and professionally, as she had decided to remain a satellite of her brother and put her musical aspirations on hold. Over the next few years her musical talents declined, moving to second soloist the next season, then finally resigning to being a member of the chorus. The demise of her brief musical career had little effect on the world of music; however, her decision would later have consequential implications to the world of astronomy.

## The Discovery of Uranus

In December of 1779, the Herschels moved from 19 New King Street to 27 Rivers Street. Along with a busy career as a conductor, William was hurriedly making telescopes and observing with them. The ever-dutiful Caroline was at William's side for both endeavors. While they lived on Rivers Street, William leased the bottom floor to a hat making business. William had bought Caroline a share of the business, but it had failed because apparently it was too far from the center of the city and the customers. On March 13, 1781, Caroline was at their old home on Rivers Street to be there for the liquidation of the shop's inventory. She wanted to ensure she was not defrauded by the other partners in the business. That very night, while Caroline was away, William took to the telescope for a night of routine double star observations. The night would turn out to be anything but routine. He spotted a star in the constellation of *Gemini* that appeared odd—it had a small but discernible disc shape. Even through the most powerful modern telescopes, stars remain as points of light, with no discernible surface evident. He was perplexed: was it a new type of star or a comet or something new altogether?

William realized his unknown new object in the sky needed confirming observations from professional astronomers to validate and possibly explain what he was seeing. To this end, he contacted through an acquaintance members of Britain's most prestigious scientific organization, the Royal Society. Two of the members, Thomas Hornsby, a professor of astronomy at Oxford, and Britain's Astronomer Royal, **Nevil Maskelyne**, began searching for the new object. A few days later the two astronomers and others confirmed William's new object. By the summer, enough observations had been taken which allowed mathematicians to calculate the orbit of the new object. The professional musician and amateur astronomer, William Herschel, had done what no one else had accomplished in all recorded history. He had added another planet to the solar system. This new planet, which orbited beyond Saturn, would later be named Uranus.

The discovery of Uranus thrust William, and by proxy Caroline, into the scientific and public eye. Almost overnight, William had gone from an amateur astronomer observing the night sky at his own whim, to a recognized astronomer who had the ear of professionals and soon King George III. William was moving from the shadows to the limelight of the British scientific community.

## The Making of an Astronomer

In May of 1782, William and Caroline's musical careers began to unwind. Her final public performance was at St. Margaret's Chapel with William at the organ and she as the treble soloist in a performance of *Messiah*. Change was coming rapidly in the Herschel family, which now consisted of William, Caroline, and occasionally their brother Andrew. William had been summoned by King George III to demonstrate his favorite telescope to the king. William's new friends in high places, such as Sir Joseph Banks, president of the Royal Society, had been privately lobbying the king to provide William with a position that would allow him to focus his talents full-time on astronomy and forsake his musical career.

In July 1782, the king granted William a modest £200 annual salary with the simple duties of living near Windsor Castle and providing observing sessions for the king and his guests upon request. Once terms were agreed upon between William and the king, William began looking for a new home near Windsor for himself and Caroline. He rented a property in the nearby village of Datchet. Then he returned to Bath, about 100 miles west of Windsor, to arrange transportation of their things. In just a few short months, Caroline's direction in life had changed drastically; no longer was she a housekeeper and musical performer, now she was to be transformed into William's astronomical assistant. There is little evidence from the letters left behind from that period that William gave any consideration to the impact this change would have on Caroline—apparently, he simply assumed her acquiescence to his new plan for her life.

William put his sister to work. In the days before the invention of the copy machine, items such as scientific papers had to be copied by hand. It was a thankless and laborious task that Caroline had mastered. She later wrote:

"My Brother was obliged to make trial of my abilities in copying for him Catalogues, Tables, &c. and sometimes whole papers which were lent him for his perusal, of which among others was one of M$^r$ Michel and a Cat. Of Christian Mayer in Latin which kept me employed when my Brother was at the Telescope at night; for when I found that a hand sometimes was wanted when any particular measures were to be made with the Lamp micrometer &c. and a fire to be kept in, and dish of Coffee necessary during a long nights watching; I undertook with pleasure what others might have thought a hardship" (Hopkins, 2007, p. 106).

Caroline was William's photocopier, word processor, and calculator all in one package.

## Caroline's "Sweeper" Telescope

To bring Caroline up to speed on observing, William built her a small refracting telescope, a type of telescope with a lens at one end of the tube and an eyepiece at the other. The tube was mounted on a vertical axis so Caroline could "sweep" horizontally around the sky for interesting objects. The instrument turned out to be awkward for her to use since she had to rotate her entire body to move about the sky.

William soon realized if he were to turn his sister into a competent and efficient observer, she would need a more functional telescope. William made for her a purpose-built sweeper of Newtonian type; that is, a telescope that has a mirror at the end of the tube that reflects the light into the eyepiece for the observer. The clever design allowed Caroline to sit virtually motionless staring through the eyepiece. She controlled the vertical angle of the telescope by pulling and later releasing control cords. She first observed with the new telescope in early July 1783. It remained her favorite instrument, and she took it with her to Hanover after William's death in 1822.

William and Caroline began to observe on a regular basis, with her in the role of William's assistant. The following day she would take the notes of the observations from the night before and update them with corrections or clarifications. On occasion she would observe independently with her smaller Newtonian sweeper telescope.

To aid them they relied on two primary sources of information about objects in the heavens. The first was the *Atlas Coelestis* prepared by the first royal astronomer, John Flamsteed. His catalog of nearly 3,000 stars was published posthumously, edited by his wife, in 1729. Though the work had its share of errors, it was the most accurate map of the heavens available at the time. The second work available was a catalog of nebulae and star clusters compiled by the French comet hunter Charles Messier. Starting in the late 1750s, Messier had started to build a list of nebulous objects in the sky that could easily be confused with a comet. By the time William obtained a copy of the catalog it had grown to 70 objects. The term "nebula" was a catch-all designation at the time that represented any fuzzy patch of light in the sky that was not a comet. Today, Messier's catalog of the brighter nebulous appearing objects, at least in a small telescope, is still in use by amateur astronomers. For example, the Messier object #57, designated M57, is also known as the Ring Nebula, and it is the glowing remains of a dying sun-like star.

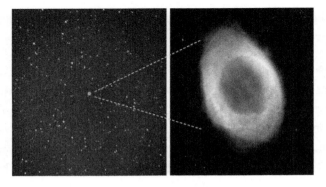

Figure – The image on the left is of M57 approximately as it would have appeared to Caroline Herschel through her small telescope (photograph by the author). The image on the right is a closeup of M57 taken with the Hubble Space Telescope.

## The Hunt for Nebulae

In February of 1783, Caroline with her small telescope and William with his larger telescope began to systematically search the sky for undiscovered nebulae and star clusters. Messier had catalogued several dozen nebulae and star clusters in his search for comets, but there were still many more to be discovered by the brother and sister pair. During 1783, Caroline recorded that she discovered 14 nebulae and clusters, and later found three more.

In the autumn of 1783 William commissioned his new 20-foot reflector telescope and began to search for nebulae and clusters. The larger telescope had an 18-inch mirror, which collected more light than his smaller telescope and allowed him to see fainter objects in the night sky. The problem became recording his observations. Once his eyes became dark adapted and he could see the faint nebulae through the eyepiece of the telescope, to record his observation he would have to write the information on paper, which required light. The light used to record his observations ruined the dark adaptation of his eyes, and it took several minutes for the pupils in his eyes to relax and allow him to see the faint objects once again. To solve the problem, William enlisted the help of Caroline. She sat at a desk near an open window throughout the night ready to record his observations as he shouted them out.

In the late summer of 1784, a French visitor at the Herschel home described Caroline at work:

"I arrived at Mr. Herschel's about ten o'clock...In stead of the master of the house, I observed, in a window at the farther end of the room, a young lady seated at a table, which was surrounded with several lights; she had a large book open before her, a pen in her hand, and directed her attention alternately to the hands of a pendulum-clock, and the index of another instrument placed beside her, the use of which I did not know. She afterwards noted down her observations.

I approached softly on tiptoe, that I might not disturb a labour, which seemed to engage all the attention of her who was engaged in it; and, have got close behind her without being observed, I found that the book she consulted was the Astronomical Atlas of Flamsteed, and that, after looking at the indexes of both the instruments, she marked, upon a large manuscript chart, points which appeared to me to indicate stars" (Hoskins, 2007, p. 111).

# Chapter 3 – Comets

In the spring of 1786 William and Caroline moved into a home located at Slough, then a small village a few miles north of Windsor. William became friends with their new neighbors, John and Mary Pitt. Mr. Pitt died that summer and William began to court Mary. At the time William was 50 and Mary was in her late 30s, about the same age as Caroline. William and Mary were married in May 1788. After the marriage, William became more involved with his wife and with the construction of a giant 40-foot telescope. William's new wife, who brought considerable wealth to the marriage, took over the role of mistress of the household, managing the servants and the family's finances. Caroline's new role as the spinster sister living in the adjoining cottage left her embittered and with time on her hands.

In July of 1786, William was sent to the observatory at Göttingen by King George III to present one of the 10-foot reflector telescopes the king had commissioned. While her brother was away, Caroline did her best to keep his observation program on track and worked on William's catalogue of nebulae that was destined for publication. With William gone, she was no longer required to work at night as his amanuensis, freeing her to pursue her own observations. She was on patrol for a previously unknown nebula to add to their catalog or possibly a comet. Her little sweeper telescope was perfect for searching large areas of the sky for the dim glow of a nebulae or for catching a glimpse of some icy new intruder from the edge of the solar system.

Her notes tell the story of her first comet discovery. She recorded on August 1: "I have calculated 100 nebulae today, and this evening I saw an object which I believe will prove tomorrow night to be a comet." The following day she recorded: "Today I calculated 150 nebulae. I fear it will not be clear to-night, it has been raining throughout the whole day, but seems now to clear up a little. 1 o'clock; the object of last night is a Comet. I did not go to rest till I had wrote to Dr. Blagden and Mr. Aubert to announce the comet."

Alexander Aubert, one of William's friends, wrote Caroline back to congratulate her on her discovery, writing: "You have immortalized your name and you deserve such a reward from the Being who has ordered all things to move as we find them." The secretary of the Royal Society, Charles Blagden, responded with his congratulations but had a request: "may wait upon you to beg the favor of viewing this phenomenon through your telescope." Caroline obliged the request and on August 6, Caroline entertained the president and secretary of the Royal Society, along with Lord Palmerston and other scientifically minded men from London who had journeyed to William's home in Slough for the sole purpose of viewing Caroline's comet through her telescope. The comet she discovered on August 1, 1786, designated today as Comet C/1786 P1, was dubbed "first lady's comet," and with it she secured her own place in the annals of the history of astronomy.

## The 40-Foot Telescope and Caroline's Salary

During construction of the 40-foot telescope, William ran out of money to finish the project. King George III had initially given William £2,000 to build the telescope; however, it turned out to not be nearly enough money. In 1787, William went back to the king for more money. The king agreed to an additional £2,000 to finish the telescope, a £200 annual stipend for maintenance of the telescope, and a small £50 salary for Caroline to work as William's assistant. Caroline was elated, as this money would give her some degree of freedom. She had always been dependent on the men in her family for her financial wellbeing, and this would give her the opportunity to earn her own way in the world. This small sum of money had the added significance that it made Caroline the first salaried woman in the history of astronomy.

By this point in her life, Caroline was an accomplished astronomer in her own right, and she did what astronomers do—observe the night sky. Using her telescope, she spent her free nights under the stars on the flat roof of her cottage meticulously sweeping the heavens for comets. These strange visitors from the edge of the solar system are rare; seldom do they become bright enough to be visible in a small telescope or to the naked eye.

Britain's Astronomer Royal, Nevil Maskelyne, visited the Herschel family and later wrote in a letter describing his visit and the telescope Caroline used: "She shewed me her 5 feet Newtonian telescope made for her by her brother for sweeping the heavens. It has an aperture of 9 inches, but magnifies only from 25 to 30 times, & takes in a field of 1° 49' being designed to shew objects very bright, for the better discovering any new visitor to our solar system, that is Comets, or any undiscovered nebula." In the letter he goes on to explain her observation method, writing, "The height of the eye-glass is altered by little in sweeping from the horizon to zenith. This she does and down again in 6 or 8 minutes, & then moves the telescope a little forward in azimuth & sweeps another portion of the heavens in like manner. She will thus sweep a quarter of the heavens in one night…Thus you see, wherever she sweeps in fine weather nothing can escape her" (Hoskin, 2011, p. 138-139).

As is the case for all comet hunters, Caroline spent many nights staring through her telescope with little to show for her efforts. She recorded her observations in a logbook that was quickly becoming full of negative entries for the elusive comets. She feared her lack of discoveries might be viewed as doing nothing to justify the king's annual salary. In a moment of discouragement she wrote, "I have kept no memorandum of my sweepings, tho' I believe I may say that I have neglected no opportunities whenever they offered; but, not meeting with any comet, I looked upon keeping memorandums of disappointments as time thrown away."

Figure – Caroline's telescope.

## Caroline's Second Comet

It was two years later before Caroline would spot another comet. She was on the hunt for a comet that had been discovered recently by the French astronomer Charles Messier. William had reckoned that the comet could be found near the astronomical North Pole. On her night off from being William's amanuensis, the chilly night of December 21, 1788, she resumed the search from two nights before. In the early morning hours, undoubtedly fatigued and tired from observing, she recorded, "When I had swept as far as Beta Lyrae, I perceived a comet." The next day Caroline sent a note to Nevil Maskelyne announcing the discovery. Caroline, William, and Maskelyne made subsequent observations of the comet until it disappeared from view in early

January of the next year. In the process of searching for Messier's comet, she found a new one of her own, not the one Messier had discovered.

One hundred and fifty-one years later, a comet was discovered on July 28, 1939, by Roger Rigollet of France. It was later confirmed from orbital calculations made by another astronomer that this was not a new comet, but rather the same one that was identified by Caroline Herschel on December 21, 1788. The comet was named 35P/1788 Y1 (Herschel-Rigollet) to honor both discoverers. Since the comet is a periodic comet, it is expected to return to the night sky in 2092.

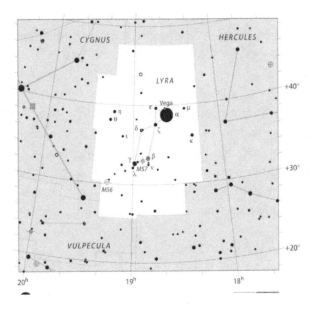

Figure – The constellation of Lyra in the northern sky.

## Caroline's Third Comet

On January 7, 1790, Caroline discovered another comet—her third. This new comet was not as easily observable as the other comets that she previously discovered, and few details were determined about it, except for its brightness of seventh magnitude (slightly fainter than the naked eye can see). In her logbook she recorded "an object with a burr all round." On January 19, with some frustration she recorded, "I have swept all evening for my comet in vain."

Around this time, William built a bigger and more powerful telescope for his sister, one that could resolve fainter objects in the night sky. The mirror was over twice the diameter, giving the telescope four times the surface area for collecting light. A drawback of this larger telescope was that the focal length was longer, making the telescope tube longer and the whole instrument more cumbersome. At just over four feet tall, Caroline had to use a step stool to peer through the eyepiece, making it uncomfortable for her to use. During her nightly observations she would use both of her telescopes, the small sweeper she looked through while sitting down and the larger instrument for fainter objects.

## Caroline's Fourth Comet

The year 1790 was a fortuitous one for Caroline Herschel. After her discovery in January, she identified another comet on April 17 and observed it until June 10. William also made confirming observations with his larger telescope. At the beginning of May the comet developed a visible tail.

One of the daunting tasks that faced 18th century astronomers was calculation of the orbit of the comet about the sun. Unlike the orbits of the planets, which are nearly circular, the orbits of comets are highly elongated, forming ellipses, parabolas, or hyperbolas. Comets with elliptical orbits become periodic and are destined to visit the inner solar system at some point in the distant future. Whereas comets with parabolic or hyperbolic orbits are one-time visitors to the inner solar system. The 17th century British astronomer Edmund Halley was the first to determine that some comets are periodic, hence Halley's comet returns every 76 years.

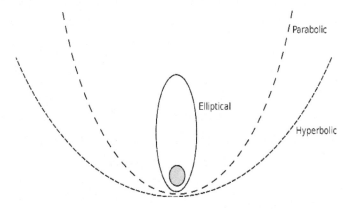

Figure – Diagram of elliptical, parabolic, and hyperbolic orbits of a comet around the sun.

## Caroline's Fifth Comet

The next comet Caroline Herschel discovered broke a 20-month hiatus during which time she was unable to find a new comet. According to Caroline, the comet she discovered on December 15, 1791, was a telescopic comet that is "pretty large." William confirmed the comet and published the discovery, giving credit to Caroline in the journal of the Royal Society, *Philosophical Transactions*.

## Caroline's Sixth Comet

Caroline discovered another comet October 7, 1793, that was barely visible to the naked eye. She was unaware that the comet had been sighted earlier by astronomer Charles Messier on September 24. The comet was thus named after Messier, given the modern name "C/1793 S2 (Messier)." Caroline officially reported on it in a letter of October 8, which was subsequently published in the journal *Philosophical Transactions*.

## Caroline's Seventh Comet

Caroline observed another comet on November 7, 1795, which was particularly bright, visible to the naked eye. It was observable for three weeks. Many astronomers trained their telescopes at the comet and its orbit was calculated, which led to the conclusion that the comet was the same object that was observed in 1786 by the French comet hunter Pierre Mechain. After the 1795 sighting, the comet was not seen again until October 19, 1805.

German astronomer Johann Encke made the orbit calculations and determined that these comets were one and the same. Encke's declaration that the comet was a periodic comet was proven when it returned in 1822 just as he predicted. As was the case with Halley's comet, the comet was named after the astronomer who determined it was periodic. It was the second periodic comet in the history of astronomy, the return of which was accurately predicted for the comet named 2P/Encke.

With the discovery of so many comets and her work on the discovery and cataloguing of nebulae, Caroline Herschel was developing a reputation in the astronomical community throughout Europe. One admirer, Professor Karl Felix Seyffer of Göttingen, wrote to her in glowing terms: "Permit me, most revered lady, to bring to your remembrance a man who has held you in the highest esteem ever since he had the good fortune to enter the Temple of Urania, at Slough, and to pay his respect to its priestess...and at the same time to express my gratitude and deepest reverence."

Figure – Image of Comet Encke obtained by Jim Scotti on January 5, 1994, while using the 0.91-meter Spacewatch Telescope on Kitt Peak.

## Caroline's Eighth and Final Comet Discovery

The last comet on Caroline Herschel's impressive list of accomplishments was discovered on August 14, 1797. It was a bright comet, clearly visible without a telescope, and she knew that others would soon spot the new intruder to the night sky. Rather than send a message by post to Maskelyne at the Greenwich Observatory, she decided to take matters into her own hands. She rode 26 miles to the observatory, six hours riding side saddle at night after just one hour of sleep. She later wrote of the adventure:

"I have so little faith in the expedition of messengers of all descriptions that I undertook to be my own...but unfortunately I undertook the task with only the preparation of one hour's sleep, and having in the course of five years never rode above two miles at a time, the twenty to London, and the idea of six or seven more to Greenwich in reserve, totally unfitted me for any action" (Hoskin, 2007, p. 115).

After excitedly reporting her observations to Maskelyne, the exhausted Caroline stayed a night or two with the Maskelynes and then began the journey back to Slough. Maskelyne urged her to call on the president of the Royal Society, Sir Joseph Banks, in London to give him the news of the discovery. Shy and demure, she declined to make the contact, stating, "I thought a woman who knows so little of the world ought not to aim at such an honour, but go home, where she ought to be, as soon as possible" (Hoskin, 2011, p. 142).

The comet was named after Herschel and Eugene Bouvard, the two astronomers who spotted it first, Comet C/1797 P1 (Bouvard-Herschel). The pair had discovered the bright comet independently within a few hours of each other. The next night, it was visible to the entire community of observers—a bright new object in the night sky.

# Chapter 4 –
# The Astronomer

For William, Caroline, and most astronomers of that day, Flamsteed's British catalogue of fixed stars was the observer's bible. It was the most accurate catalog of the position of the stars known, with nearly 3,000 stars. It was the first star catalog based on observations with a telescope and was the culmination of Britain's first Astronomer Royal John Flamsteed's life's work. Though the catalog was the best at the time, it had problems. As a result of observer's errors, or copyists or printer's mistakes, the catalog was riddled with errors. In 1795 William recommended that Caroline turn her attention to cleaning up the defects in the star atlas.

The meticulous work of cross referencing, indexing the multivolume catalog, and comparing it to her brother's observations came naturally for Caroline. After two years of work, she had found 561 stars that had been omitted from the British Catalogue by mistake. Maskelyne publicly recognized Caroline's work, acknowledging that observers could now use the catalogue with full confidence in the work, and he persuaded the Royal Society to pay for the publication of the revised catalogue. She was thrilled with the accolades for her work, telling Maskelyne: "...flattered my vanity not a little. You see, Sir, I do own myself to be vain because I would not wish to be singular, and was there ever a woman without vanity?—or a man either? Only with this difference, that among gentlemen the commodity is generally stiled ambition" (Hoskin, 2007, p. 116).

## Birth of John Herschel

In her early 40s, Mary Herschel gave birth to what would be her and William's only child, John. The child brought a bit of happiness into Caroline's life, a world that was nearly devoid of human affection. The boy helped heal the wound Caroline suffered over her brother's marriage to Mary, who she felt had taken her brother from her. Over the years, as William and Mary traveled extensively, Caroline was put in charge of William's household and her young nephew. As John matured into an accomplished man, he still remained affectionate to his doting aunt.

## Caroline Leaves Slough

For reasons that are not clear, toward the end of 1797 Caroline moved from her cottage at Slough. Apparently, she left in haste, as she lodged temporarily with one of the workmen and his wife. She eventually lived in a series of rental properties in the Windsor area. Moving away from William and Mary's home made her night sessions working with her brother as the amanuensis more complicated as she now needed one of the workmen to escort her home late into the night. Her daytime task of refining the previous night's observations and editing catalogues of stars and nebulae was problematic as she seemed to always be short the one reference book or paper that she needed. Decades later she wrote, "For the last 24 years of my living in England, it was amongst beings of whom I was afraid...I was obliged to change my habitation no less than 7 times, which was always attended by useless expenses, and what was still more precious, loss of time..." (Hoskin, 2007, p. 117).

## Dietrich

Caroline found that William, 12 years her senior, was not someone to whom she could pour out her deepest feelings, later writing that she "kept to the resolution of never opening my lips to my dear brother William about worldly or serious concerns." However, her younger brother Dietrich was another story. She had always had a special affection for him, and he came for a pleasant visit in the summer of 1806 to see his English family. He returned to England within two years, this time under very different circumstances. The power struggle between the French General Napoleon and the King of Prussia had made it hard for Dietrich to support his family in Hanover, so out of desperation he moved to Bath to find work and sent money home to his wife and children. He ended up staying in England for five years. To help with the support of Dietrich's family, Caroline was generous with what money she had.

For a time, Caroline's personal world was in order. Her brothers William, Alexander, and Dietrich were in

England as well as her dear friend Mme. Beckedorff, whom she had known since childhood. In 1812, things slowly began to change. Dietrich went back to Hanover, Alexander retired there in 1816, and her friend also returned to Hanover upon her retirement. By now, John was in his 20s, consumed with science and moving in the upper circles of the London scientific community, which left little time for his dear aunt. The innumerable cold damp nights spent under the stars had taken their toll on William's health, leaving him often sick and seldom at the telescope. As her world changed, she began to think of her life after William and made a plan for a return to Hanover to be with her family and old friends.

Her brother Alexander died in 1821, but this changed little of her plan to return to Hanover. She would still have Dietrich and his family. Dietrich always seemed to be short on money, and Caroline helped with her meager income. Added to Dietrich's problems was the fact that his daughter Sophia's husband was "deranged," and she and her children were destitute. To show her commitment to Dietrich and his family, Caroline gave her savings of £500 to him. In late August 1822, William finally succumbed to old age and his infirmities. Caroline and the family were devastated by his death for he had been the mainstay of the tight-knit family. His passing hastened Caroline's plans to return to Hanover.

# Chapter 5 -
# Return to Hanover

After the death of William, Caroline was overwhelmed with grief. She had lost her purpose in life. Her nephew John was fully into an astronomical collaboration with his friend James South on the study of double stars. John was more involved with the Royal Society and the Astronomical Society than his father had been and spent much of his time in London, seldom visiting Slough. Her only living sibling was Dietrich, who was in Hanover. After living in England for half a century, most of her life, she made the decision to return to Hanover to live with Dietrich and his family. A decision she would later regret.

Just days after William's death, Caroline set the wheels in motion for the move to Hanover. Slough had too many bittersweet memories for her to stay. Shortly after William's funeral she began to dispose of her furniture, keeping a small portion to take with her. In a letter to a friend, John tells of his aunt's condition, "She has resolved on leaving England immediately and going to reside with her family in Hanover, and the expectation of preparing for her journey has been of service in distracting her attention from dwelling on its cause" (Hoskin, 2007, p. 122). John urged her to wait until his father's affairs were settled and he could escort her to

Hanover. Instead, Dietrich travelled to England to escort his sister to her new home.

Upon arrival in Hanover, Caroline was accepted into Dietrich's family, but discord soon arose. Caroline was convinced that the only reason she was there was for the money she had provided and now they wanted to extract every last pence from her. She began to resent Dietrich's family and regret that she had cast her lot with what she would later describe as "a mongrel breed."

## Nebula Catalog

From Hanover she continued to refine the catalog of nebulae that she and William worked on for all those years. John was now a competent astronomer and was busy continuing his father's work. John and a fellow observer, James South, had diligently followed up with observations of double stars started by William. Next John began to systematically observe the 2,500 objects in the Herschel catalog of nebulae. The problem was that the catalog was ordered by class and the date of discovery, a format that was cumbersome for John's follow-up observations. To aid John in his work, Caroline organized the catalog of nebulae based upon their distance from the astronomical North Pole. This allowed John to systematically observe the objects in the catalog, making corrections and clarifications as required. Caroline completed the onerous task in 1825, producing a catalog of 104 folio pages of numbers.

Though her personal world was in disarray, the greater world of astronomy began to pay homage to a woman that had contributed so much to science. Her awards and honors were numerous, including the Gold Medal of the Royal Astronomical Society in 1828. In 1832, her discoveries in the field of astronomy were honored by the king of Denmark with a medal. She was named an Honorary Member of the Royal Irish Academy in Dublin in 1838, and three years before that she was named an Honorary Member of the Royal Astronomical Society in Britain. Herschel and Mary Somerville were the first women to be accepted into this prestigious organization. On her 96th birthday in 1846, Caroline Herschel was awarded the Gold Medal for Science by the king of Prussia.

Her beloved nephew John visited her three times during her remaining years in Hanover. The first visit came just two years after she arrived, when John was returning to England from one of his European tours. They discussed what would be the ideal format for the catalog of nebulae that Caroline was working on for John. He returned in 1832 and must have discussed with her his plans for his upcoming trip to the Cape of Good Hope to map the southern sky. He found his 82-year-old aunt in good spirits, later writing, "I found my aunt wonderfully well and very nicely and comfortably lodged, and we have since been on the full trot. She runs about the town with me and skips up her two flights of stairs as light and fresh at least as some folks I could name who are not a fourth part of her age…" (Hoskin, 2011, p. 197).

After four years of observing and recording the southern sky, John returned to Britain with great fanfare, being given the hereditary title of baronet by Queen Victoria. On his journey home from Africa in 1838, he once again stopped in Hanover to visit Caroline and brought with him his young son William. Caroline was elated to see the young boy, realizing that he would carry the family name forward. At age 88, Caroline feared that this would probably be the last time she would see John and prepared a speech of final farewell. John, not willing to face the finality of the situation, departed quietly with his son without Caroline's knowledge.

At age 94 she wrote to John's wife to see how John's reductions of the observations he had taken at Cape Town were progressing. The process of reducing his observations taken in South Africa to the universal astronomical coordinate system were laborious and took John years to complete. Caroline knew that if the observations were not put in a format where other astronomers could use them, they would be of little value. Finally, in the summer of 1847, when Caroline was into her ninety-seventh year, John's volume entitled *Result of Astronomical Observations Made...at the Cape of Good Hope, Being a Completion of a Telescopic Survey of the Whole of the Visible Heavens, Commenced in 1825* arrived. Thus, John had fulfilled his promise to his father to continue his work and became the first observer in history, and probably the last, to examine the entire celestial sphere visually with a major telescope. At her advanced age she was unable to write, but she must have been filled with joy to see the fulfillment of the Herschel family legacy finally in print.

Just a few months after receiving John's masterwork, on January 9, 1848, Caroline's body succumbed to the ravages of time. At her funeral, the king of Hanover and the crown prince and princess sent their coaches to follow the hearse as a mark of respect. By order of the crown princess, Caroline's coffin was adorned with palm branches. Caroline had requested that a copy of the almanac used by her father and a lock of William's hair be placed in her coffin.

Figure – Caroline Herschel at about age 97.

## Legacy of Caroline Herschel

In recognition of her tremendous contributions to astronomy, both as an assistant to her brother and as an astronomer in her own right, the scientific community honored Caroline Herschel by immortalizing her name. Aside from the comets that bear her name, there is a crater on the moon called "C. Herschel" and an asteroid (Asteroid 281) discovered in 1888 that is named "Lucretia."

Caroline Herschel was a pioneer in her field. Deprived of a formal education and limited by poor health in her early life, she accepted the role her mother assigned to her as a maid, but she took the opportunity to better herself when she was given the chance. She was a trailblazer in the field of astronomy, making discoveries of previously unknown heavenly objects and producing painstakingly complex mathematical calculations by hand. For hundreds of years, she has and will continue to be an inspiration for young women to pursue a life in science. She held the record for having the most comet discoveries by a woman until Carolyn Shoemaker usurped her in the 1980s. All can take inspiration from the amazing journey and long productive life of this strong woman and accomplished astronomer.

# Timeline of the Life and Times of Caroline Herschel

November 15, 1738 - Friedrich Wilhelm (William) Herschel born in Hanover, Germany.

March 16, 1750 - Caroline Lucretia Herschel born in Hanover, Germany.

Fall 1757 – Jacob and William flee to England. French forces occupy Hanover during the Seven Years War.

Spring 1764 – William returns to Hanover for a visit. Caroline completes education at Garrison school and is confirmed at church.

August 24, 1772 – Caroline arrives in England to live with William in Bath.

October 1779 – William begins a systematic survey of the heavens for double stars.

March 13, 1781 – William discovers the planet Uranus.

1782 – Caroline gives her final musical performance.

August 1782 – William and Caroline move into a house at Datchet, near Windsor Castle.

1783 – Caroline becomes William's astronomical assistant. She detects three new nebulae.

June 1785 – William and Caroline move to a house in Clay Hall in Old Windsor.

1786 – William and Caroline move into a house at Slough on Windsor Road.

1787 – Caroline receives £50 annual salary from King George III to be William's astronomical assistant.

1786 to 1797 – Caroline discovers eight comets.

May 8, 1788 – William marries the widow Mrs. Mary Pitt.

March 7, 1792 – John Herschel is born to William and Mary Herschel.

1798 – Caroline presents to the Royal Society an Index to Flamsteed's observations and a catalog of 560 stars omitted form the British Catalogue.

1822 – Caroline completes catalog of 2,500 nebula and star clusters.

August 25, 1822 – William dies.

1828 – Caroline is awarded the Gold Medal of the Royal Astronomical Society.

January 9, 1848 – Caroline dies in Hanover.

# Biographical Sketches

Flamsteed, John (1646 - 1719) was the first British Astronomer Royal. As a young man John Flamsteed had poor health and was forced to leave school early. As a result, he educated himself at home. His scientific career began under the tutelage of William Brouncker, the first president of the Royal Society. King George II appointed Flamsteed as the first Astronomer Royal with the task of building the Royal Greenwich Observatory, which opened in 1675. From the observatory he measured and recorded the position of over 3,000 stars. After his death his observations were published in the *Historia coelestis Britannica* (British Celestial Record). It was the first great modern telescopic catalog and established Greenwich as one of the leading observatories in the world.

Herschel, John (1792 - 1871) was a British scientist and astronomer. John Herschel was born in Slough, England, the son of the famous astronomer William Herschel. John was educated primarily by private tutors during his youth until he entered Cambridge University. There he earned first place in the university mathematics examinations. In 1816, he began to assist his father in astronomical research. Additionally, he made important contributions to chemistry, the physics of light, and mathematics, for which he was awarded the prestigious Copley Medal of the Royal Society. As an astronomer,

Herschel, in collaboration with James South, re-observed the catalog of double stars that his father had developed. In 1833, John and his family set sail for the Cape of Good Hope in South Africa with a 20-foot telescope to observe and record the stars of the southern hemisphere. After four years he returned to England with a large catalog of observations. He was made a baronet in 1838 and was lionized by the scientific community. During the 1840s he worked on reduction of his observations from South Africa and wrote a textbook on astronomy, which was the standard text for decades. In 1860 he was appointed master of the British Mint.

Figure – John Herschel in 1833.

Herschel, William (1738 – 1822) was a British scientist and astronomer. William Herschel was born in Hanover (in present-day Germany) and moved to England in 1757 where he worked as an itinerant musician until he settled in Bath. His sister Caroline Herschel joined him in Bath in 1772. He became very interested in astronomy, built his own telescopes, and discovered the planet Uranus in 1781. The discovery brought the attention of King George III, who appointed him the astronomer to the king with an annual salary of £200. With the financial backing of the king, William built a 40-foot reflecting telescope, then the largest telescope in the world. Herschel, with the help of his sister, was a prodigious observer and cataloguer of the double stars and nebulae in the night sky. During his career he cataloged over 800 double stars and 2,000 nebulae. He also discovered additional moons of Saturn, two moons of Uranus, and infrared radiation. He was the first to attempt to understand the structure of the universe. In recognition of his contributions, Herschel was awarded the Copley Medal by the Royal Society in 1821, also elected as a Fellow of the Royal Society, and his name is associated with the Herschel Space Observatory, which was launched in 2009.

Figure – William Herschel in 1785.

<u>Maskelyne, Nevil</u> (1732 – 1811) was the fifth British Astronomer Royal, holding the office from 1865 to 1811. Nevil Maskelyne graduated from Trinity College, Cambridge, in 1754. He was ordained in the Anglican Church and received a position at a church near London; however, he spent much of his time assisting the Astronomer Royal James Bradley. Maskelyne was elected a fellow of Trinity College in 1758 and of the Royal Society the following year. In 1761 he was sent to observe the transit of Venus, from which the distance of the Earth from the sun can be calculated. He went on a second voyage to Barbados to assess the accuracy of rival chronometer methods of longitude determination.

In 1774, he was the first person to scientifically measure the Earth's density, hence its mass, by measuring deviations in gravitational effects of Mt. Schiehallion, in Scotland. As British Astronomer Royal he supervised the work of the annual *Nautical Almanac* until his death.

## The End

Thank you for purchasing this book. I hope you enjoyed reading it. Please don't forget to leave a review of the book. I read each one and they help me become a better writer.

-Doug

# References and Further Reading

*A Dictionary of Scientists*. Oxford: Oxford University Press, 1999.

Brock, Claire. *The Comet Sweeper: Caroline Herschel's Astronomical Ambition*. London: Icon Books Ltd., 2017.

Gillispie, Charles C. *Dictionary of Scientific Biography*. New York: Charles Scribner's Sons, 1980.

Hoskin, Michael (Editor). *Caroline Herschel's Autobiographies*. Cambridge: Science History Publications Ltd, 2003.

Hoskin, Michael. *Discoverers of the Universe: William and Caroline Herschel*. Princeton, New Jersey: Princeton University Press, 2011.

Hoskin, Michael. *The Herschels of Hanover*. Cambridge: Science History Publications Ltd, 2007.

Lemonick, Michael D. *Georgian Star: How William and Caroline Herschel Revolutionized Our Understanding of the Cosmos*. New York: W.W. Norton & Company, Inc., 2009.

Olson, Roberta J.M. and Jay Pasachoff. "The Comets of Caroline Herschel (1750-1848), Sleuth of the Skies at Slough." December 2012. Accessed November 20, 2022. https://www.researchgate.net/publication/233824443_Th

e_Comets_of_Caroline_Herschel_1750-1848_Sleuth_of_the_Skies_atSlough

West, Doug. *The Astronomer William Herschel: A Short Biography*. Missouri: C&D Publications, 2023.

Yeomans, Donald K. *Comets: A Chronological History of Observation, Science, Myth, and Folklore*. New York: John Wiley & Sons, Inc., 1991.

# Acknowledgements

I would like to thank Cynthia West, Lisa Zahn, and the Linda Hall Library for their help in the preparation of this book. All the photographs are from the public domain.

# About the Author

Doug West is a retired engineer and experienced non-fiction writer with several books to his credit. His writing interests are general, with expertise in science, history, and biographies. Doug has a B.S. in Physics from the Missouri School of Science and Technology and a Ph.D. in General Engineering from Oklahoma State University. He is a member of the American Association of Variable Star Observers (AAVSO) and Astronomical Society of Kansas City. He lives with his wife and little dog "Millie" near Kansas City, Missouri. Additional books by Doug West can be found at https://www.amazon.com/Doug-West/e/B00961PJ8M. Follow the author on Facebook at:
https://www.facebook.com/30minutebooks and at
https://30minutebookseries.com.

Figure – Doug West.

# Additional Books in the 30 Minute Book Series

All books are by Doug West unless otherwise noted.

A Short Biography of the Scientist Sir Isaac Newton

A Short Biography of the Astronomer Edwin Hubble

Galileo Galilei – A Short Biography

Benjamin Franklin – A Short Biography

The American Revolutionary War – A Short History

The Astronomer Cecilia Payne-Gaposchkin – A Short Biography

Dr. Walter Reed – A Short Biography by Erin Delong

Coinage of the United States – A Short History

John Adams – A Short Biography

Alexander Hamilton – A Short Biography

The Great Depression – A Short History

Jesse Owens, Adolf Hitler and the 1936 Summer Olympics

Thomas Jefferson – A Short Biography

The French and Indian War – A Short History

The Mathematician John Forbes Nash, Jr. – A Short Biography

Vice President Mike Pence – A Short Biography

President Jimmy Carter – A Short Biography

President Ronald Reagan – A Short Biography

President George H. W. Bush – A Short Biography

Dr. Robert H. Goddard – A Brief Biography - Father of American Rocketry and the Space Age

Richard Nixon: A Short Biography - 37th President of the United States

Charles Lindbergh: A Short Biography - Famed Aviator and Environmentalist

Dr. Wernher von Braun: A Short Biography - Pioneer of Rocketry and Space Exploration

Bill Clinton: A Short Biography – 42nd President of the United States

Joe Biden: A Short Biography - 47th Vice President of the United States

Donald Trump: A Short Biography - 45th President of the United States

Nicolaus Copernicus: A Short Biography - The Astronomer Who Moved the Earth

America's Second War of Independence: A Short History of the War of 1812

John Quincy Adams: A Short Biography - Sixth President of the United States

Andrew Jackson: A Short Biography: Seventh President of the United States

Franklin Delano Roosevelt: A Short Biography: Thirty-Second President of the United States

James Clerk Maxwell: A Short Biography: Giant of Nineteenth-Century Physics

Ernest Rutherford: A Short Biography: The Father of Nuclear Physics

Sir William Crookes: A Short Biography: Nineteenth-Century British Chemist and Spiritualist

The Journey of Apollo 11 to the Moon

William Henry Harrison: A Short Biography: Tenth President of the United States

John Tyler: A Short Biography: Eleventh President of the United States

James K. Polk: A Short Biography: Eleventh President of the United States

Samuel Adams: A Short Biography: Architect of the American Revolution

The Mexican-American War: A Short History: America's Fulfillment of Manifest Destiny

History of the Plymouth and Massachusetts Bay Colonies: Pilgrims, Puritans, and the Founding of New England

The History of the Jamestown Colony: America's First Permanent English Settlement

Zachary Taylor: A Short Biography: Twelfth President of the United States

Herbert Hoover: A Short Biography: Thirty-First President of the United States

The Great 1929 Stock Market Crash: A Short History

Christopher Columbus and the Discovery of the Americas

The Formation of the 13 Colonies in America: A Short History

Religion in Colonial America: A Short History

George Washington: A Short Biography: First President of the United States

Dr. Benjamin Rush: A Short Biography: Physician and Founding Father of America

The 1918 Spanish Flu Pandemic in America: A Short History

The Ancient Milesian Philosophers: Thales, Anaximander, Anaximenes: A Short Introduction to Their Lives and Works

Martha Washington: First Lady of the United States: A Short Biography

The First Continental Congress: A Short History

Dwight D. Eisenhower: A Short Biography: 34th President of the United States

The American-British Artist Benjamin West: A Short Biography

Abigail Adams: First Lady of the United States: A Short Biography

The Seven Kings of Ancient Rome: A Short Introduction

John Bartram: Colonial America's Premier Botanist: A Short Biography

The Astronomer Tycho Brahe: A Short Biography

William Penn: The Founder of Pennsylvania: A Short Biography

Writing of the Declaration of Independence: A Short History

Dolley Madison: First Lady of the United States: A Short Biography

# Index

Printed in Great Britain
by Amazon

26005318R00040